DANIIL KARABUT

The Secret Lives of Trees

Exploring Their Communication, Cooperation, and Significance

Copyright © 2023 by Daniil Karabut

All rights reserved. No part of this publication may be reproduced, stored or transmitted in any form or by any means, electronic, mechanical, photocopying, recording, scanning, or otherwise without written permission from the publisher. It is illegal to copy this book, post it to a website, or distribute it by any other means without permission.

Daniil Karabut asserts the moral right to be identified as the author of this work.

First edition

This book was professionally typeset on Reedsy.
Find out more at reedsy.com

"Trees are the earth's endless effort to speak to the listening heaven."

       Rabindranath Tagore

Contents

Foreword	ii
Acknowledgement	iii
Chapter 1: Introduction to the World of Trees	1
Chapter 2: Communication and Cooperation Among Trees	6
Chapter 3: Adaptations of Trees to Their Environment	9
Chapter 4: Trees and Climate Change	12
Chapter 5: The Cultural and Historical Significance of Trees	15
Chapter 6: The Future of Trees	18
Epilogue	21

Foreword

Trees are some of the most fascinating and complex organisms on our planet. They play a vital role in maintaining the health and stability of our ecosystems, providing countless benefits to humans and all other living beings.

As we face pressing environmental challenges such as climate change, deforestation, and habitat loss, it is more important than ever that we understand and appreciate the importance of trees in our world. This book provides an informative and engaging overview of the world of trees, covering everything from their communication and cooperation systems to their historical and cultural significance.

Through exploring the wonders of trees, this book reminds us of our planet's intricate and interconnected nature and the importance of our responsibility to protect and preserve the natural world for future generations. I hope readers of this book will come away with a greater appreciation for the wonder of trees and their role in our world and be inspired to take action to protect and preserve these essential organisms.

Acknowledgement

I want to express my gratitude to the many individuals who have contributed to the creation of this book.

First and foremost, I would like to thank my family and friends for their unwavering support and encouragement throughout this journey. Their love and encouragement have been a constant source of inspiration.

I would also like to thank the researchers, scholars, and writers whose work has contributed to our understanding of the importance of trees in our world. Their insights and discoveries have been instrumental in shaping the content of this book.

I am also grateful to the trees and forests worldwide, whose presence and contributions to our planet have inspired me to write this book.

Finally, I would like to thank the readers of this book. I hope that this book will inspire you to appreciate the wonder of trees and their importance in our world and to take action to protect and preserve them for future generations.

Chapter 1: Introduction to the World of Trees

Trees are some of the most important organisms on our planet. They play a vital role in our ecosystems, providing habitat and food for countless species, maintaining soil health and preventing erosion, and cycling water and nutrients through the environment.

Trees are often called the "lungs of the earth" because they absorb carbon dioxide from the atmosphere and release oxygen through photosynthesis. Without trees, our air would be much less breathable, and our planet would be a much less hospitable place for humans and other animals to live.

But the importance of trees goes beyond their role in the ecosystem. Trees also have immense cultural and spiritual significance for many human societies, and they have been used for food, medicine, shelter, and fuel for thousands of years.

Despite their significance, however, many of us take trees for granted. We may appreciate their beauty and shade, but we may not fully understand their vital role in our lives and our planet's health.

This book will explore the world of trees, from their intricate communication systems to their remarkable survival strategies. We will examine the impact of climate change on trees and their crucial role in mitigating its effects. We will also consider trees' cultural and historical significance, including their use in art, mythology, and religion.

Throughout this journey, we will gain a deeper appreciation of the beauty and complexity of the natural world and the critical role that trees play in sustaining life on Earth.

* * *

The Importance of Trees in the Ecosystem

Trees are among the most important organisms on our planet, and their presence is vital to the health and balance of our global ecosystem. As we explore the world of trees in this book, it is essential to understand their fundamental importance to life on Earth.

Trees are the primary producers in many ecosystems, meaning that they convert sunlight into organic matter that other organisms can use for energy. This process, known as photosynthesis, allows trees to absorb carbon dioxide from the atmosphere and release oxygen, thus producing the clean air we breathe.

In addition to their role in the carbon and oxygen cycles, trees also play a critical role in regulating the water cycle. Trees absorb water through their roots and release it into the air through transpiration, which helps cool the air and generate precipitation. This process is critical in regions with arid or semi-arid climates, where trees can help to prevent desertification and maintain healthy soil.

But the importance of trees goes beyond their role in the global ecosystem. Trees also provide habitat and food for countless species, from the tiniest insects to the largest mammals. They

CHAPTER 1: INTRODUCTION TO THE WORLD OF TREES

act as natural barriers to wind and water erosion and help maintain the soil's balance by stabilizing slopes and preventing runoff.

Furthermore, trees are an essential resource for human societies, providing us with food, medicine, building materials, and fuel. For thousands of years, they have been used for these purposes and are crucial in sustaining many rural communities worldwide.

Despite their significance, trees face various threats in the modern world, from deforestation and habitat loss to climate change and pollution. In the following chapters of this book, we will explore these and other challenges facing trees and the strategies being developed to protect and preserve them for future generations.

Overall, the importance of trees to the ecosystem and human society cannot be overstated. By understanding these remarkable organisms and their role in our world, we can better appreciate their value and work towards creating a more sustainable and equitable future for ourselves and all living beings on Earth.

* * *

The world of trees is incredibly diverse, with a wide range of species that vary in shape, size, and ecological niche. Understanding the essential characteristics of trees can help us appreciate their importance and complexity.

A critical distinction between trees is their method of reproduction. Some trees reproduce through seeds, while others reproduce through vegetative propagation, such as growing from shoots or cuttings. Trees can also be classified based on their life cycle, with deciduous trees losing their leaves seasonally and evergreen trees retaining them year-round.

Physical characteristics also vary among tree species. Hardwood trees, such as oak and maple, have dense hardwood used for furniture and flooring, while softwood trees, such as pine and spruce, have lighter wood used for construction and paper production. Some trees grow tall and straight, while others have a more bushy or spreading growth pattern. Certain trees have thorns or other defensive structures, while others have smooth bark or a distinctive fragrance.

The ecological niche is another essential characteristic of trees. Some trees are shade tolerant and can grow in the understory of a forest, while others require full sunlight to thrive. Some trees are adapted to wetlands or other waterlogged environments, while others can survive in dry conditions.

In summary, the world of trees is incredibly diverse, with many species and characteristics. Understanding these characteristics is essential for appreciating the importance and complexity of trees in our ecosystem and daily lives.

* * *

Brief History of Human Interactions with Trees

Humans have had a long and complex relationship with trees, dating back thousands of years. Trees have been used for various purposes, from providing food and shelter to serving as fuel and building materials.

Trees have also played an important role in mythology and folklore in many cultures. Trees have been seen as symbols of strength, wisdom, and spirituality and are associated with various gods and goddesses in different religions.

In prehistoric times, humans relied heavily on trees for their survival. They used trees for shelter, building boats and other structures, fuel, and tools. Some early societies also developed methods of preserving food using the bark of certain tree species.

As human societies developed, using trees became more complex and sophisticated. In medieval Europe, for example, forests were managed as a resource, with certain trees designated for specific purposes, such as shipbuilding or charcoal production.

During the colonial era, trees were crucial in developing new territories, with forests cleared for agriculture, logging, and other uses. This led to widespread deforestation and habitat loss, profoundly impacting the natural world.

In recent years, there has been a growing awareness of the importance of trees for our planet's health and the well-being of human societies. Many efforts have been made to protect and preserve forests and to promote sustainable forestry practices.

In summary, the history of human interactions with trees is a long and complex one, reflecting our evolving relationship with the natural world. By understanding this history, we can better appreciate trees' vital role in our lives and our planet's health. We can also work towards a more sustainable and equitable future where trees are valued and protected for their crucial ecological, cultural, and spiritual significance.

Chapter 2: Communication and Cooperation Among Trees

The Complex Communication Systems of Trees, Including Chemical Signals and Networks of Fungi

Trees are not just individual organisms but are part of complex networks of communication and cooperation that allow them to survive and thrive in their environments.

One of the most remarkable aspects of tree communication is their ability to release chemical signals into the air or soil that can signal danger or attract beneficial organisms. For example, when insects or diseases attack a tree, it can release chemicals that warn neighboring trees of the threat, allowing them to activate their defense mechanisms. Trees can also release chemicals that attract beneficial insects, such as pollinators, or that help to repel predators.

In addition to chemical signals, trees can communicate through fungi networks that grow in association with their roots. These networks, known as mycorrhizal networks, allow trees to share resources and information, such as water, nutrients, and genetic material.

Trees can support each other through these networks during stress, such as drought or nutrient-poor soil conditions. They can also transfer resources to weaker or younger trees, helping them to survive and grow.

The complexity of tree communication and cooperation is remarkable and is just beginning to be fully understood by scientists. As we continue to explore the world of trees, we will gain a deeper appreciation for the interconnectedness of all life on our planet and its crucial role in sustaining it.

* * *

How trees cooperate with other species in the forest

Trees are not solitary organisms but part of complex and interdependent ecosystems. Within these ecosystems, trees cancan collaborate with other species in various ways that promote the health and resilience of the entire ecosystem.

One way in which trees cooperate is through sharing resources. Trees can exchange nutrients and water through their roots and transfer resources to weaker or younger needy trees. This helps to ensure that all trees in the ecosystem can thrive and contribute to the health of the entire forest.

Trees also work together to create and maintain the physical structure of the forest. By growing tall and straight, some trees provide a canopy that shades the forest floor, reducing competition for resources and creating a microclimate beneficial for a wide range of plant and animal species.

Furthermore, trees can cooperate with other species in the forest by providing habitat and food for various animals, from insects to mammals. Some trees also have symbiotic relationships with fungi, which help to break down organic matter and make nutrients available to the tree and other organisms in the ecosystem.

Through these cooperative relationships, trees can promote

the health and resilience of the entire forest ecosystem. This underscores the importance of protecting and preserving not just individual trees but entire forest ecosystems, which are crucial to the health and well-being of our planet.

Chapter 3: Adaptations of Trees to Their Environment

The Different Ways that Trees Adapt to Their Environment, Including Changing Leaf Shape and Developing Defensive Mechanisms Against Predators

Trees can adapt to various environments, from the hottest deserts to the coldest tundras. This adaptability is due to multiple mechanisms trees have developed over millions of years of evolution.

One way in which trees adapt to their environment is by changing the shape and structure of their leaves. For example, in hot, arid climates, trees may have smaller, thicker leaves that can retain moisture more effectively. In colder environments, trees may have more extensive, broader leaves that absorb more sunlight and generate more energy.

Another way in which trees adapt is by developing defensive mechanisms against predators. Some trees have thorns or other structures that deter animals from eating their leaves or bark, while others produce chemicals that make their leaves unpalatable or toxic. Some trees can also respond to insect attacks by producing extra resin or sap, which can trap or suffocate the insects.

In addition to these specific adaptations, trees can adjust their growth and development in response to environmental cues. For example, trees in cold climates may go into dormancy during the winter months, conserving energy until the warmer weather returns. Trees in wet environments may develop specialized roots that can extract oxygen from the soil, allowing them to survive in anaerobic conditions.

The adaptability of trees is a testament to these organisms' remarkable resilience and resourcefulness. As we learn more about how trees adapt to their environment, we can gain a deeper appreciation for the complexity and diversity of the natural world. We can also work towards creating a more sustainable and equitable future where we protect and preserve these remarkable organisms for future generations.

* * *

The Role of Trees in Preventing Soil Erosion and Maintaining Healthy Ecosystems

Trees play a crucial role in maintaining the health and stability of ecosystems by preventing soil erosion and promoting healthy soil conditions.

One way in which trees prevent soil erosion is by stabilizing slopes and preventing runoff. The root systems of trees help to hold soil in place, reducing the likelihood of landslides and erosion caused by rain or wind. Trees also help slow water movement across the landscape, allowing it to soak into the ground and replenish groundwater reserves.

In addition to preventing erosion, trees help maintain healthy soil conditions by cycling nutrients and organic matter through the ecosystem. When trees shed leaves or other organic matter, they decompose on the forest floor, enriching the soil and providing nutrients for other organisms.

Trees can also improve soil quality by promoting the growth of beneficial microorganisms, such as fungi and bacteria, which help break down organic matter and make nutrients available to other plants in the ecosystem. Through these processes, trees help create and maintain healthy, nutrient-rich soil crucial for the growth and survival of various plant and animal species.

Furthermore, trees can support biodiversity by providing habitat and food for various species, from insects to mammals. They help to create and maintain complex ecosystems that can sustain a wide range of life forms, promoting resilience and stability in the face of environmental changes and disturbances.

Trees are crucial in preventing soil erosion and maintaining healthy ecosystems. By understanding the importance of trees in these processes, we can work towards creating a more sustainable and equitable future where we protect and preserve these remarkable organisms for future generations.

Chapter 4: Trees and Climate Change

The Impact of Climate Change on Trees and Their Ability to Adapt

Climate change significantly impacts the world's forests and the trees that inhabit them. Rising temperatures, changes in precipitation patterns, and increased frequency of extreme weather events affect tree species' growth, reproduction, and survival worldwide.

One of the most significant impacts of climate change on trees is the disruption of seasonal patterns. Trees rely on seasonal cues, such as temperature and daylight, to determine when to leaf out, flower, and set seed. Many tree species struggle to adapt as temperatures rise and seasonal patterns err.

In addition to changing seasonal patterns, climate change is also affecting the availability of water, which is crucial for the survival of trees. Drought conditions are becoming more common in many parts of the world, leading to stress and death for many tree species. Changes in precipitation patterns also affect water availability for trees, with some areas experiencing increased flooding or prolonged periods of dryness.

Despite these challenges, trees can adapt to changing environmental conditions. Many tree species can adjust their growth and development in response to changing climate patterns, such

CHAPTER 4: TREES AND CLIMATE CHANGE

as by shifting their range or altering their leaf shape or timing of leaf emergence. Some tree species may also be able to evolve new traits that allow them to adapt better to changing conditions over time.

However, the ability of trees to adapt is limited by the rate and severity of climate change and other stressors such as habitat loss and fragmentation, disease, and invasive species. Therefore, we must take action to mitigate the impacts of climate change and protect and preserve forest ecosystems for future generations.

In summary, climate change significantly impacts the world's forests and the trees that inhabit them. By understanding the challenges that trees face in adapting to changing environmental conditions, we can work towards creating a more sustainable and resilient future for these remarkable organisms and the ecosystems they inhabit.

* * *

The Role of Trees in Mitigating Climate Change Through Carbon Sequestration and Other Methods

While climate change has significantly impacted trees, trees also play a crucial role in mitigating climate change through carbon sequestration and other methods.

Carbon sequestration is how trees absorb and store carbon dioxide from the atmosphere. Trees cancan do this through photosynthesis, using sunlight to convert carbon dioxide into organic matter, which is stored in their leaves, branches, and trunks.

Through this process, trees can remove significant amounts of carbon dioxide from the atmosphere, helping to reduce the concentration of greenhouse gases that contribute to climate change. In addition to carbon sequestration, trees also provide other benefits that help to mitigate climate change, such as reducing soil erosion, maintaining healthy soil conditions, and providing a habitat for a wide range of plant and animal species.

Forests also have the potential to play a significant role in mitigating climate change through forest management practices that promote sustainable forestry. Sustainable forestry practices, such as reducing deforestation, promoting reforestation, and improving forest management, can help increase carbon sequestration in forests while providing economic and social benefits to local communities.

In addition to these direct benefits, trees and forests can also help reduce climate change's impacts by providing shade and cooling, reducing the urban heat island effect, and mitigating the impacts of extreme weather events, such as flooding and landslides.

Trees and forests are crucial in mitigating climate change through carbon sequestration and other methods. By understanding the importance of trees in mitigating climate change, we can work towards creating a more sustainable and resilient future for our planet and its inhabitants.

Chapter 5: The Cultural and Historical Significance of Trees

The Role of Trees in Human Culture, Including Myths, Folklore, and Religious Traditions

Trees have played a central role in human culture and history, with many cultures and religions associating trees with spiritual and symbolic significance worldwide.

In many cultures, trees have been seen as symbols of life, growth, and renewal. They have been associated with creation myths, such as the world tree in Norse mythology, and depicted in art and literature as sources of inspiration and spiritual connection.

Trees have also been used in religious traditions and rituals, such as in the practice of the Christmas tree in Christianity and the Bodhi tree in Buddhism. In some cultures, trees have been worshipped as sacred beings, with offerings and prayers made to them as a sign of respect and gratitude.

In addition to their spiritual significance, trees have played an important role in folklore and storytelling. Trees have been depicted as characters in many stories and legends, such as the Ents in J.R.R. Tolkien's "The Lord of the Rings" and the World Tree Yggdrasil in Norse mythology.

Furthermore, trees have been used for practical purposes

in many cultures, providing food, shelter, fuel, and building materials. In some societies, trees have also been used for medicinal purposes, with various parts of the tree used to treat a wide range of ailments.

Trees' cultural and historical significance underscores humans' deep and complex relationship with the natural world. By understanding trees' cultural and spiritual sense, we can gain a deeper appreciation for their importance in our lives and work towards creating a more sustainable and equitable future where trees are valued and protected for their crucial ecological, cultural, and spiritual significance.

* * *

The Historical Importance of Trees in Human Societies, Including Their Use for Building, Medicine, and Other Purposes

Trees have been a vital resource for human societies throughout history, providing many materials and resources for practical use. One of the most important uses of trees has been for building, with various parts of the tree used for construction materials, such as timber, planks, and beams. Trees have also been used for making furniture, tools, and other household items.

In addition to building materials, trees have been used for medicinal purposes in many societies. Various parts of the tree, such as the bark, leaves, and roots, have been used for their healing properties, with traditional herbal remedies based on the use of trees still in use today.

Trees have also been used for food and fuel, with many societies relying on the fruits, nuts, and seeds of trees for sustenance. Trees have also been used for power, with wood and

CHAPTER 5: THE CULTURAL AND HISTORICAL SIGNIFICANCE OF TREES

charcoal being essential energy sources for cooking and heating.

Furthermore, trees have played an essential role in developing many cultures and societies, with certain trees and forests considered sacred or culturally significant. Some organizations have used trees as a means of communication and recording history, with trees being used as markers or signs to denote actual events or locations.

In many ways, the historical importance of trees in human societies underscores the deep and complex relationship humans have with the natural world. By understanding the role of trees in our history and culture, we can gain a deeper appreciation for their importance in our lives and work towards creating a more sustainable and equitable future where trees are valued and protected for their crucial ecological and cultural significance.

Chapter 6: The Future of Trees

The Challenges and Opportunities Facing Trees in the Modern World

The future of trees is facing many challenges in the modern world, but there are also opportunities to create a more sustainable and equitable future for these remarkable organisms.

One of the most significant challenges trees face is habitat loss and fragmentation caused by deforestation, urbanization, and other human activities. This loss of habitat can lead to a reduction in biodiversity and can negatively impact the ability of trees to sequester carbon and provide other ecosystem services.

Another major challenge facing trees is climate change, which is causing changes in temperature and precipitation patterns affecting the growth and survival of tree species worldwide. As temperatures rise and weather patterns become more erratic, many tree species struggle to adapt, decreasing forest health and productivity.

In addition to these challenges, trees face other stressors, such as invasive species, disease, and pollution. These stressors can reduce the health and resilience of forest ecosystems, making them more vulnerable to further environmental disturbances.

Despite these challenges, opportunities exist to create a more sustainable and equitable future for trees. Sustainable forestry practices, such as reducing deforestation and promoting reforestation, can help increase the health and productivity of forest ecosystems while providing economic and social benefits to local communities.

In addition to sustainable forestry practices, there are also opportunities to use trees and forests to mitigate climate change through carbon sequestration and other ecosystem services. By protecting and preserving forests, we can also help to maintain the biodiversity and cultural significance of these ecosystems, ensuring that they continue to provide essential benefits to future generations.

In summary, trees' challenges and opportunities in the modern world underscore the need for a more sustainable and equitable approach to forest management and conservation. By working together to protect and preserve these remarkable organisms, we can create a more resilient and sustainable future for our planet and its inhabitants.

* * *

Strategies for Protecting and Preserving Forests and Individual Trees for Future Generations

Protecting and preserving forests and individual trees is crucial for ensuring a sustainable and healthy future for our planet and its inhabitants. Here are some strategies that can be used to protect and preserve forests and individual trees for future generations:

1. Sustainable forestry practices: Sustainable forestry practices, such as reducing deforestation and promoting reforestation, can help increase the health and productivity

of forest ecosystems while providing economic and social benefits to local communities. These practices can include selective logging, forest thinning, and prescribed burning.
2. Conservation and restoration: Conserving and restoring forests can help protect biodiversity, maintain ecosystem services, and provide habitats for various plant and animal species. This can be achieved through protected areas, habitat corridors, and restoration projects.
3. Education and awareness: Educating the public about the importance of forests and individual trees can help to raise awareness and promote conservation efforts. This can include public outreach programs, community involvement, and education campaigns.
4. Policy and legislation: Governments can play a crucial role in protecting and preserving forests and individual trees through policy and legislation. This can include laws and regulations that protect forests from development, promote sustainable forestry practices, and provide incentives for conservation and restoration efforts.
5. Community involvement: Local communities can also be essential in protecting and preserving forests and individual trees. This can include community-based forest management, land trusts, and partnerships between communities and conservation organizations.

By implementing these strategies, we can work towards creating a more sustainable and equitable future for forests and individual trees, ensuring that they continue to provide essential benefits to future generations.

Epilogue

Personal Reflections on the Author's Experiences and Observations of Trees

As I reflect on the wonder of trees and their importance in our world, I am struck by their incredible resilience and adaptability in changing environmental conditions. From their complex communication networks to their ability to sequester carbon and promote healthy ecosystems, trees are genuinely remarkable organisms that play a crucial role in maintaining the health and stability of our planet.

Throughout my life, I have had the privilege of observing and experiencing the beauty and majesty of trees firsthand. Whether hiking through a dense forest or walking through a city park, the presence of trees has always brought me a sense of calm and connection to the natural world.

I have also witnessed the impact of human activities on trees and forests, from deforestation and habitat loss to the effects of climate change. These experiences have highlighted our urgent need to protect and preserve these remarkable organisms for future generations.

As I conclude this book, I am left with a deep appreciation for the importance of trees in our world and a renewed commitment to working towards a more sustainable and equitable future for these remarkable organisms. By valuing and protecting trees and forests, we can create a healthier and more resilient planet where trees continue to provide essential benefits to all living beings.

Printed in Great Britain
by Amazon